JESUS AND TRUMP

The Parallel Sayings

JESUS AND TRUMP

The Parallel Sayings

INTRODUCTION BY JAMES ADAMS

GALT BOOKS

JESUS AND TRUMP: THE PARALLEL SAYINGS

Copyright © 2025 Galt Books

All rights reserved. Any unauthorized duplication in whole or in part or dissemination of this edition by any means (including but not limited to photocopying, electronic devices, digital versions, and the internet) will be prosecuted to the fullest extent of the law.

Scripture quotations marked (NIV) are taken from the Holy Bible, New International Version®, NIV®. Copyright © 1973, 1978, 1984, 2011 by Biblica, Inc.™ Used by permission of Zondervan. All rights reserved worldwide. www.zondervan.com The "NIV" and "New International Version" are trademarks registered in the United States Patent and Trademark Office by Biblica, Inc.™

Scripture quotations marked (NLT) are taken from the Holy Bible, New Living Translation, copyright ©1996, 2004, 2015 by Tyndale House Foundation. Used by permission of Tyndale House Publishers, Carol Stream, Illinois 60188. All rights reserved.

Printed in China.

ISBN: 9781965290071

First edition 2025

INTRODUCTION

Throughout history, humanity has sought leaders—figures who inspire, challenge, and transform the world around them. For Christians, Jesus Christ is the ultimate model of leadership, truth, and divine purpose. His words, recorded in Scripture, have been quoted for centuries as the foundation for moral and spiritual guidance. Yet, in modern times, political leaders often capture a similar spotlight, commanding the attention, loyalty, and even reverence of their followers. Among them, one figure has emerged with an undeniably unique voice, a voice that has ignited fierce devotion, intense controversy, and unwavering discussion: Donald J. Trump.

At first glance, comparing the words of Jesus with those of Donald Trump may seem audacious, even provocative. What possible parallels could exist between the teachings of a first-century rabbi who preached humility, love, and salvation, and the statements of a 21st-century businessman-turned-politician, whose rhetoric often appears bold, brash, and unapologetically combative? Yet this book, *Jesus & Trump: The Parallel Sayings*, takes on that very exploration—not to equate the two men or their missions but to highlight their commonalities in language, tone, and the unexpected resonance their words have with their respective followers.

The Gospels tell us that Jesus spoke to his audience with an authority unlike anyone they had heard before. He challenged religious elites, upended societal norms, and connected with ordinary people in deeply personal ways. His sayings—"I am the way, the truth, and the life," "Blessed are the meek," "Love your enemies"—were radical, inspiring, and often polarizing. His words stirred the hearts of his followers and enraged his opponents, leaving no one indifferent.

Donald Trump, too, speaks with an authority that is unconventional, direct, and unmistakably his own. Like Jesus, he upends expectations, defies traditional norms, and creates a stark division among those who hear him. His supporters view him as a truth-teller, someone who "says what others won't say" and stands against the powerful elites. His critics see his statements as inflammatory, controversial, and even dangerous. And yet, Trump's words—whether spoken in speeches, interviews, or tweets—have had a profound effect on his followers, eliciting a loyalty that mirrors the intensity of faith itself.

This book is not intended to judge either figure but to present their words side by side, allowing readers to observe the parallels, contrasts, and striking connections that arise. From themes of leadership, loyalty, and truth to messages of conflict, authority, and redemption, *Jesus & Trump* reveals how their sayings—separated by two millennia—resonate with similar undertones and provoke similarly powerful responses.

Some may read this book and find humor in the comparison; others may be unsettled, surprised, or deeply reflective. Regardless of where one stands politically or spiritually, this collection challenges us to consider the weight of words and the extraordinary influence of those who speak them. Words can build or destroy, unite or divide. Whether divine or human, their impact lingers, shaping how people live, think, and act.

Jesus & Trump: The Parallel Sayings is not just a book about two men—it is a study of how language can create movements, inspire action, and forge legacies that endure long after the speakers have departed from the world stage. Let the words speak for themselves.

Trump

"I alone can fix it."

Republican National Convention, July 21, 2016

JESUS

"His light brought life to everyone."

(John 1:4 NLT)

Trump

"Think big and live large."

Trump: How to Get Rich, 2004

JESUS

"My purpose is to give them a rich and satisfying life."

(John 10:10 NLT)

Trump

"We will make America great again."

Inaugural Address, January 20, 2017

JESUS

"The kingdom of God has come near."

(Mark 1:15 NIV)

Trump

"The forgotten men and women will be forgotten no longer."

Inaugural Address, January 20, 2017

JESUS

"The last will be first, and the first will be last."

(Matthew 20:16 NIV)

Trump

"The best is yet to come."

State of the Union Address, February 4, 2020

JESUS

"I am making everything new!"

(Revelation 21:5 NIV)

Trump

"Together, we will determine the course of America and the world for years to come."

Inaugural Address, January 20, 2017

JESUS

"And you will be my witnesses, telling people about me everywhere—in Jerusalem, throughout Judea, in Samaria, and to the ends of the earth."

(Acts 1:8 NLT)

Trump

"Promises made, promises kept."

Victory speech, November 6, 2024

JESUS

"Heaven and earth will pass away, but my words will never pass away."

(Matthew 24:35 NIV)

Trump

"In the end, you're measured not by how much you undertake, but by what you finally accomplish."

New York Magazine, 1987

JESUS

"By their fruit, you will recognize them."

(Matthew 7:20 NIV)

Trump

"Together, we will win."

Campaign rally in Colorado Springs,
Colorado, February 20, 2020

JESUS

"Where two or three gather in my name, there am I with them."

(Matthew 18:20 NIV)

TRUMP

"Be a warrior for the truth."

Commencement Address at Liberty
University, May 13, 2017

JESUS

"You will know the truth, and the truth will set you free."

(John 8:32 NIV)

Trump

Together, we will make our nations stronger, our countries safer, our culture richer...

Speech at World Economic Forum, Davos, Switzerland, January 21, 2020

JESUS

"God blesses those who are persecuted for doing right, for the Kingdom of Heaven is theirs."

(Matthew 5:10 NLT)

Trump

"We overcame obstacles that nobody thought possible."

Victory speech, November 6, 2024

JESUS

"With man this is impossible, but with God all things are possible."

(Matthew 19:26 **NIV**)

Trump

"...together there is nothing Americans can't do..."

Commencement Speech at US Naval Academy, May 25, 2018

JESUS

"God causes everything to work together for the good of those who love God."

(Romans 8:28 NLT)

Trump

"We must all work together to lift each other up. Working, building, restoring together."

Campaign rally in Charlotte, North Carolina, October 14, 2016

Jesus

"A cord of three strands is not quickly broken."

(Ecclesiastes 4:12 **NIV**)

Trump

"We have to rebuild our infrastructure."

"Legislative Outline for Rebuilding Infrastructure in America," Trump White House Archives

JESUS

"First wash the inside of the cup and the dish, and then the outside will become clean, too."

(Matthew 23:26 NLT)

Trump

"No dream is too big, no challenge is too great. Nothing we want for our future is beyond our reach."

Victory Speech, November 9, 2016

JESUS

"In this world you will have trouble. But take heart! I have overcome the world."

(John 16:33 NIV)

Trump

"Let us bring light to their lives one by one and empower them to light up the world."

Speech at the World Economic Forum in Davos, Switzerland, January 21, 2020

JESUS

"The light shines in the darkness, and the darkness has not overcome it."

(John 1:5 NIV)

TRUMP

"Freedom unifies the soul."

State of the Union Address, February 4, 2020

JESUS

"If the Son sets you free, you will be free indeed."

(John 8:36 NIV)

Trump

"We will not bend, we will not break, we will not yield."

Speech at the North Carolina Republican Convention, June 5, 2021

JESUS

"The one who stands firm to the end will be saved."

(Matthew 24:13 NIV)

Trump

"We will stand up to the radical left lunatics."

Speech at rally in Youngstown, Ohio, September 17, 2022

Jesus

"Watch out for false prophets. They come to you in sheep's clothing, but inwardly they are ferocious wolves."

(Matthew 7:15 **NIV**)

Trump

"I am the world's greatest person."

Phone conversation with the Australian Prime Minister Malcolm Turnbull, January 27, 2017

JESUS

"I am the way, the truth, and the life."

(John 14:6 NLT)

Trump

"Many of the leaks coming out of the White House are fabricated lies made up by the fake news media."

Twitter post, May 28, 2017

Jesus

"But woe unto you, scribes and Pharisees, hypocrites!"

(Matthew 23:13 NIV)

Trump

"I'm the most persecuted person in the history of our country."

Rally in Waukesha, Wisconsin, August 5, 2022

JESUS

"If the world hates you, remember that it hated me first."

(John 15:18 NLT)

Trump

"Whether you love me or hate me, you have to vote for me."

Rally in New Hampshire, August 15, 2019

JESUS

"Anyone who isn't with me opposes me, and anyone who isn't working with me is actually working against me."

(Matthew 12:30 NLT)

Trump

"We're going to drain the swamp."

2016 Campaign slogan

JESUS

"I have come to bring fire on the earth, and how I wish it were already kindled!"

(Luke 12:49 **NIV**)

Trump

"I am the chosen one."

CNBC, August 21, 2019

JESUS

"I have been given all authority in heaven and on earth."

(Matthew 28:18 NLT)

Trump

"As long as we have faith in each other and trust in God, then there is no goal at all beyond our reach."

Statement to CPAC, February 25, 2017

JESUS

"Anything is possible if a person believes."

(Mark 9:23 NLT)

Trump

"I am inclined to pardon many of them. I can't say for every single one because a couple of them, probably, they got out of control."

CNN, May 11, 2023

JESUS

"Father, forgive them, for they do not know what they are doing."

(Luke 23:34 NLT)

Trump

"I like thinking big. If you're going to be thinking anything, you might as well think big."

Facebook post, November 21, 2016

JESUS

"Don't be afraid; you are worth more than many sparrows."

(Luke 12:7 NIV)

Trump

"I think I've made a lot of sacrifices. I work very, very hard."

ABC News, July 30, 2016

Jesus

"It is more blessed to give than to receive."

(Acts 20:35 NLT)

Trump

"Now it's time for America to bind the wounds of division. We have to get together. To all Republicans and Democrats and independents across this nation, I say it is time for us to come together as one united people."

Presidential acceptance speech, November 9, 2016

JESUS

"Do to others as you would like them to do to you."

(Luke 6:31 NLT)

Trump

"Together, we will have one great American future. We will be one people, under one God, saluting one American flag."

Speech in Philadelphia, September 7, 2016

JESUS

"Come, follow me, and I will show you how to fish for people!"

(Matthew 4:19 NLT)

Trump

"A new national pride will stir our souls, lift our sights, and heal our division."

Inaugural Address, January 20, 2017

JESUS

"I will come and heal him."

(Matthew 8:7 NLT)

Trump

"I am your voice."

Campaign speech, July 21, 2016

JESUS

"Follow me."

(Matthew 9:9 NIV)

Trump

"Don't be afraid of it. You're going to beat it."

CBS News, October 6, 2020

JESUS

"Don't be afraid," he said. "Take courage. I am here!"

(Matthew 14:27 NLT)

Trump

"The American dream is dead. But if I win, I will bring it back bigger and better and stronger than ever before."

Campaign announcement speech, June 16, 2015

JESUS

The Spirit of the Lord is on me, because he has anointed me to proclaim good news to the poor. He has sent me to proclaim freedom for the prisoners and recovery of sight for the blind, to set the oppressed free."

(Luke 4:18 NIV)

TRUMP

"We must choose to believe in America. History is watching us now."

Republican National Convention acceptance speech, July 21, 2016

JESUS

"According to your faith let it be done to you."

(Matthew 9:29b NIV)

Trump

"I like to hire people that I've seen in action. I often hire people that were on the opposing side of a deal that I respect."

The Washington Post, September 23, 1989, as quoted in The World According to Trump, *2005*

JESUS

"His master replied, 'Well done, good and faithful servant! You have been faithful with a few things; I will put you in charge of many things. Come and share your master's happiness!'"

(Matthew 25:21 NLT)

Trump

"Our movement is about replacing a failed and corrupt political establishment with a new government controlled by you, the American people."

Donald Trump's Argument for America
TV ad, November 4, 2016

Jesus

"For the Kingdom of God is already among you."

(Luke 17:21b NLT)

Trump

"We're going to win so much you may even get tired of winning."

Campaign rally in Albany, NY, April 11, 2016

JESUS

"Those who are victorious will sit with me on my throne, just as I was victorious and sat with my Father on his throne."

(Revelation 3:21 NLT)

Trump

"I have made the tough decisions, always with an eye toward the bottom line. Perhaps it's time America was run like a business."

The World According to Trump: An Unauthorized Portrait in His Own Words, 2005

JESUS

"A faithful, sensible servant is one to whom the master can give the responsibility of managing his other household servants and feeding them."

(Matthew 24:45 NLT)

Trump

"We will no longer surrender this country, or its people, to the false song of globalism."

Foreign policy speech, April 27, 2016

JESUS

"No one can serve two masters. Either you will hate the one and love the other, or you will be devoted to the one and despise the other."

(Matthew 6:24 NIV)

Trump

"We will follow two simple rules: buy American and hire American."

Inaugural Address, January 20, 2017

JESUS

"Stay there, eating and drinking whatever they give you, for the worker deserves his wages. Do not move around from house to house."

(Luke 10:7 NIV)

Trump

"From this day forward, a new vision will govern our land. From this moment on, it's going to be America first."

Inaugural Address, January 20, 2017

JESUS

"And upon this rock I will build my church, and all the powers of hell will not conquer it."

(Matthew 16:18b NLT)

Trump

"The nation-state remains the true foundation for happiness and harmony."

Foreign policy speech, April 27, 2016

JESUS

"Seek the Kingdom of God above all else, and live righteously, and he will give you everything you need."

(Matthew 6:33 NLT)

Trump

"No longer will we enter into these massive deals, with many countries, that are thousands of pages long and which no one from our country even reads or understands."

Republican National Convention acceptance speech, July 2, 2016

Jesus

"All you need to say is simply 'Yes' or 'No'; anything beyond this comes from the evil one."

(Matthew 5:37 NIV)

Trump

"You can't be scared. You do your thing, you hold your ground, you stand up tall, and whatever happens, happens."

Trump: The Art of the Deal, 1987

JESUS

"Do not be afraid of those who kill the body but cannot kill the soul."

(Matthew 10:28 NIV)

Trump

"I'm not a politician, thank goodness. Politicians are all talk, no action."

Conservative Political Action Conference, February 27, 2015

Jesus

"Not everyone who calls out to me, 'Lord! Lord!' will enter the Kingdom of Heaven. Only those who actually do the will of my Father in heaven will enter."

(Matthew 7:21 NLT)

Trump

"What separates the winners from the losers is how a person reacts to each new twist of fate."

Trump: Surviving at the Top, 1990

JESUS

"Anyone who listens to my teaching and follows it is wise, like a person who builds a house on solid rock. Though the rain comes in torrents and the floodwaters rise and the winds beat against that house, it won't collapse because it is built on bedrock."

(Matthew 7:24-25 NLT)

Trump

"You know, I'm like a smart person."

Fox News interview, December 11, 2016

Jesus

"Now someone greater than Solomon is here."

(Matthew 12:42 NLT)

Trump

"The fake news media . . . is not my enemy, it is the enemy of the American people!"

Twitter post, February 17, 2017

JESUS

"You belong to your father, the devil, and you want to carry out your father's desires. He was a murderer from the beginning, not holding to the truth, for there is no truth in him. When he lies, he speaks his native language, for he is a liar and the father of lies."

(John 8:44 NIV)

Trump

Trump: "The wall just got 10 feet taller."

Republican Presidential Debate, February 26, 2016

JESUS

"Do you think I came to bring peace on earth? No, I tell you, but division."

(Luke 12:51 **NIV**)

Trump

"It's called extreme vetting."

Presidential Debate, October 9, 2016

Jesus

"But small is the gate and narrow the road that leads to life, and only a few find it."

(Matthew 7:14 NIV)

Trump

"Our government leaders and our media have totally lost touch with the people."

Campaign speech, Jackson, Mississippi, August 24, 2016

Jesus

"The teachers of the law and the Pharisees sit in Moses' seat. So you must be careful to do everything they tell you. But do not do what they do, for they do not practice what they preach."

(Matthew 23:2-3 NIV)

Trump

"America is a nation of believers, dreamers, and strivers that is being led by a group of censors, critics, and cynics."

Republican National Convention acceptance speech, July 21, 2016

Jesus

"You shut the door of the kingdom of heaven in people's faces. You yourselves do not enter, nor will you let those enter who are trying to."

(Matthew 23:13 NIV)

Trump

"The media has been unbelievably dishonest. I mean they'll take a statement that you make, which is perfect, and they'll cut it up and chop it up."

RT America interview, September 8, 2016

JESUS

"You hypocrites, why are you trying to trap me?"

(Matthew 22:18 NIV)

Trump

"I inherited a mess. It's a mess. At home and abroad, a mess."

Press conference, February 16, 2017

Jesus

"O Jerusalem, Jerusalem, the city that kills the prophets and stones God's messengers! How often I have wanted to gather your children together as a hen protects her chicks beneath her wings, but you wouldn't let me."

(Matthew 23:37 NLT)

Trump

"Sad to see the history and culture of our great country being ripped apart with the removal of our beautiful statues and monuments."

Twitter post, August 17, 2017

JESUS

"Yes, look at these great buildings. But they will be completely demolished. Not one stone will be left on top of another!"

(Mark 13:2 NLT)

Trump

"We will be one people, under one God, saluting one American flag. And we will be a nation of generosity and warmth. But we will also be a nation of law and order. There is salvation for America."

Presidential nomination acceptance speech, July 21, 2016

JESUS

"Truly I tell you, today you will be with me in paradise."

(Luke 23:43 NIV)